T0358118

# FOR
# Weddings
## *and a*
# FUNERAL

# John Marsden

# For Weddings *and a* Funeral

........................

*SPECIAL POEMS FOR SPECIAL OCCASIONS*

MACMILLAN
Pan Macmillan Australia

John Marsden can be visited at his website:

http://www.macmillan.com.au/pma/marsden


First published 1996 in Macmillan by Pan Macmillan Australia Pty Limited
St Martins Tower, 31 Market Street, Sydney

Reprinted 1998, 2000, 2002

Introduction © John Marsden 1996
For copyright in individual poems see Acknowledgements p. 141

Every endeavour has been made to contact copyright holders to obtain the necessary
permission. Any copyright holder who has been inadvertently overlooked should
contact the publisher.

All rights reserved. No part of this book may be reproduced or
transmitted in any form or by any means, electronic or
mechanical, including photocopying, recording or by any
informational storage and retrieval system, without prior
permission in writing from the publisher.

National Library of Australia
cataloguing-in-publication data:

For weddings and a funeral
ISBN 0 7329 0852 3

1. English poetry. 2. Weddings–poetry. 3. Funeral rites and ceremonies–poetry. I.
Marsden, John, 1950- .

821.0080354

Typeset in 12/13 Perpetua by Midland Typesetters
Printed by IVE

MIX
Paper from
responsible sources
FSC
www.fsc.org
FSC® C018183

*To Sarah Vickers-Willis*

*Thanks to Roos and Jeanne Marsden,*
*Sarah Vickers-Willis,*
*Charlotte and Rick Lindsay.*

# ❖ CONTENTS ❖

CONTENTS

CONTENTS

## *AND* A Funeral

# ❖ INTRODUCTION ❖

Suddenly a whole lot of people started asking me for poems!

It began with friends who were getting married. They wanted a poem for their wedding: a special poem that would have special meaning for them. Something they would remember forever.

It sounded simple. I've always been a big fan of poetry. I read a lot of it. I have a large collection of poetry books. But it wasn't easy at all. There aren't too many poems that lend themselves to weddings. After a long search I re-discovered an old favourite: 'Ithaca' by C.P. Cavafy.

Luckily they loved it. Read at the wedding by a family member who had some acting experience, it created a memorable moment for everybody.

The next request was just a week later. It was for a poem that could be read at a funeral; the funeral of a dear friend who died suddenly at the age of fifty. I offered the family 'Do not stand at my grave and weep'.

As the requests kept coming I realised that we were seeing a new social phenomenon. Poetry was 'hot' again, maybe due to films like Four Weddings and a Funeral, where Matthew reads W.H. Auden's 'Stop All the Clocks', and Hannah and Her Sisters, where Michael Caine quotes E.E. Cummings with such grace and beauty.

But equally hot is our desire to acknowledge the uniqueness of each of our relatives and friends. It's not surprising, of course. As we learn to value individuals and individuality so we become dissatisfied with 'the same' for everyone. Sometimes the people who officiate at the important ceremonies in our lives sound a little stale, a little tired, as they read again the words they have read a thousand times before. It can be important for everyone who takes part in ceremonies to have something chosen specifically for the occasion.

Poets have always had a special ability to express our deepest feelings in the most moving and effective language. It is a great gift that they offer us.

It is my hope that everyone who reads this book will accept that gift.

JOHN MARSDEN

# FOR
# *Weddings*

❖ ❖ ❖

# THE OWL AND THE PUSSY-CAT

EDWARD LEAR

The Owl and the Pussy-Cat went to sea
   In a beautiful pea-green boat:
They took some honey, and plenty of money
   Wrapped up in a five-pound note.
The Owl looked up to the stars above,
   And sang to a small guitar,
'O lovely Pussy, O Pussy, my love,
   What a beautiful Pussy you are,
     You are,
     You are!
   What a beautiful Pussy you are!'

Pussy said to the Owl, 'You elegant fowl,
   How charmingly sweet you sing!
Oh! let us be married; too long we have tarried:
   But what shall we do for a ring?'
They sailed away, for a year and a day,
   To the land where the bong-tree grows;
And there in a wood a Piggy-wig stood,
   With a ring at the end of his nose,
     His nose,

❖

His nose,
With a ring at the end of his nose.

'Dear Pig, are you willing to sell for one shilling
Your ring?' Said the Piggy, 'I will.'
So they took it away, and were married next day
By the Turkey who lives on the hill.
They dined on mince and slices of quince,
Which they ate with a runcible spoon;
And hand in hand, on the edge of the sand,
They danced by the light of the moon,
The moon,
The moon,
They danced by the light of the moon.

# MARRIED LOVE

KUAN TAO-SHENG
*Translated by Kenneth Rexroth and Ling Chung*

❖

You and I
Have so much love
That it
Burns like a fire,
In which we bake a lump of clay
Molded into a figure of you
And a figure of me.
Then we take both of them,
And break them into pieces,
And mix the pieces with water,
And mold again a figure of you,
And a figure of me.
I am in your clay.
You are in my clay.
In life we share a single quilt.
In death we will share one bed.

# 'LET ME NOT TO THE MARRIAGE OF TRUE MINDS'

WILLIAM SHAKESPEARE

Let me not to the marriage of true minds
Admit impediments. Love is not love
Which alters when it alteration finds,
Or bends with the remover to remove:
O, no! it is an ever-fixèd mark,
That looks on tempests and is never shaken;
It is the star to every wandering bark,
Whose worth's unknown, although its height be
    taken.
Love's not Time's fool, though rosy lips and
    cheeks
Within his bending sickle's compass come;
Love alters not with his brief hours and weeks
But bears it out even to the edge of doom.
    If this be error and upon me proved,
    I never writ, nor no man ever loved.

# PROTHALAMION

## MAY SARTON

❖

How pure the hearts of lovers as they walk
Through the rich quiet fields
Where the stiff wheat grows heavy on the stalk
And over barley and its paler golds
The air is bright—

They do not even walk yet hand in hand,
But every sense is pricked alive so sharp
That life breathes through them from the
    burning land
And they could use the wind itself for harp,
And oh, to drink the light!

Now all around them earth moves toward an end,
The gold turning to bronze, the barley tasseled,
The fruit stored up, and soon the sheaves will bend
Their heads together in the rich wedding-bed
All are about to enter.

❖

The hearts of lovers as they walk, how pure;
How cool the wind upon the open palm
As they move on toward harvest, and so sure
Even this ripening has a marvellous calm
And a still center.

# 'MY HEART IS LIKE A SINGING BIRD'

### CHRISTINA ROSSETTI

My heart is like a singing bird
  Whose nest is in a watered shoot:
My heart is like an apple-tree
  Whose boughs are bent with thickset fruit;
My heart is like a rainbow shell
  That paddles in a halcyon sea;
My heart is gladder than all these
  Because my love is come to me.

Raise me a dais of silk and down;
  Hang it with vair and purple dyes;
Carve it in doves and pomegranates,
  And peacocks with a hundred eyes;
Work it in gold and silver grapes,
  In leaves and silver fleurs-de-lys;
Because the birthday of my life
  Is come, my love is come to me.

# 'NOW YOU WILL FEEL NO RAIN'

APACHE SONG
*Translator unknown*

Now you will feel no rain,
for each of you will be a shelter to the other.

Now you will feel no cold,
for each of you will be warmth to the other.

Now there is no loneliness for you;
now there is no more loneliness.

Now you are two bodies,
but there is only one life before you.

Go now to your dwelling place,
to enter into your days together.

And may your days be good
and long on the earth.

# AT THE WEDDING MARCH

## GERARD MANLEY HOPKINS

God with honour hang your head,
Groom, and grace you, bride, your bed
With lissome scions, sweet scions,
Out of hallowed bodies bred.

Each be other's comfort kind:
Déep, déeper than divined,
Divine charity, dear charity,
Fast you ever, fast bind.

Then let the March tread our ears:
I to him turn with tears
Who to wedlock, his wonder wedlock,
Déals tríumph and immortal years.

# 'WILD NIGHTS—WILD NIGHTS!'

## EMILY DICKINSON

Wild Nights—Wild Nights!
Were I with thee
Wild Nights should be
Our luxury!

Futile—the Winds—
To a Heart in port—
Done with the Compass—
Done with the Chart!

Rowing in Eden—
Ah, the Sea!
Might I but moor—Tonight—
In Thee!

# 'NO LOVE, TO LOVE OF MAN AND WIFE'

RICHARD EEDES

No love, to love of man and wife;
No hope, to hope of constant heart;
No joy, to joy in wedded life;
No faith, to faith in either part:
    Flesh is of flesh, and bone of bone
    When deeds and words and thoughts are one.

Thy friend an other friend may be,
But other self is not the same:
Thy spouse the self-same is with thee,
In body, mind, in goods and name:
    No thine, no mine, may other call,
    Now all is one, and one is all.

# THE SUN RISING

JOHN DONNE

Busy old fool, unruly Sun,
　　Why dost thou thus,
Through windows and through curtains call on us?
Must to thy motions lovers' seasons run?
　　Saucy pedantic wretch, go chide
　　Late school-boys, and sour 'prentices,
　Go tell court-huntsmen that the King will ride,
　Call country ants to harvest offices;
Love, all alike, no season knows, nor clime,
Nor hours, days, months, which are the rags of time.

　　Thy beams, so reverend and strong
　　Why shouldst thou think?
I could eclipse and cloud them with a wink,
But that I would not lose her sight so long:
　　If her eyes have not blinded thine,
　　Look, and tomorrow late tell me,
　Whether both the Indias of spice and mine
　Be where thou left'st them, or lie here with me.
Ask for those kings whom thou saw'st yesterday,
And thou shalt hear, 'All here in one bed lay.'

❖

She's all States, and all Princes I;
    Nothing else is.
Princes do but play us; compared to this,
All honour's mimic; all wealth alchemy.
    Thou, Sun, art half as happy as we,
    In that the world's contracted thus;
  Thine age asks ease, and since thy duties be
  To warm the world, that's done in warming us.
Shine here to us, and thou art everywhere;
This bed thy centre is, these walls thy sphere.

# AN HOUR WITH THEE

### SIR WALTER SCOTT

❖

An hour with thee! When earliest day
Dapples with gold the eastern grey,
Oh, what can frame my mind to bear
The toil and turmoil, cark and care,
New griefs, which coming hours unfold,
And sad remembrance of the old?
   One hour with thee.

One hour with thee! When burning June
Waves his red flag at pitch of noon;
What shall repay the faithful swain,
His labour on the sultry plain;
And, more than cave or sheltering bough,
Cool feverish blood and throbbing brow?
   One hour with thee.

One hour with thee! When sun is set,
Oh, what can teach me to forget
The thankless labours of the day;
The hopes, the wishes, flung away;
The increasing wants, and lessening gains,
The master's pride, who scorns my pains?
   One hour with thee.

# CURFEW

PAUL ÉLUARD
*Translated from the French by Quentin Stevenson*

What else could we do, for the doors were
   guarded,
What else could we do, for they had
   imprisoned us,
What else could we do, for the streets were
   forbidden us,
What else could we do, for the town was
   asleep?
What else could we do, for she hungered and
   thirsted,
What else could we do, for we were
   defenceless,
What else could we do, for night had
   descended,
What else could we do, for we were in love?

# 'IF I HAVE MADE,
# MY LADY, INTRICATE'

E.E. CUMMINGS

if i have made, my lady, intricate
imperfect various things chiefly which wrong
your eyes(frailer than most deep dreams are frail)
songs less firm than your body's whitest song
upon my mind—if i have failed to snare
the glance too shy—if through my singing slips
the very skilful strangeness of your smile
the keen primeval silence of your hair

—let the world say 'his most wise music stole
nothing from death'—

               you only will create
(who are so perfectly alive)my shame:
lady through whose profound and fragile lips
the sweet small clumsy feet of April came

into the ragged meadow of my soul.

# BEAUTY

## WILLIAM SHAKESPEARE

❖

When in the chronicle of wasted time
I see descriptions of the fairest wight,
And beauty making beautiful old rhyme
In praise of ladies dead, and lovely knights;

Then in the blazon of sweet beauty's best
Of hand, of foot, of lip, of eye, of brow,
I see their antique pen would have exprest
Ev'n such a beauty as you master now.

So all their praises are but prophecies
Of this our time, all, you prefiguring;
And for they look'd but with diving eyes,
They had not skill enough your worth to sing:

For we, which now behold these present days,
Have eyes to wonder, but lack tongues to praise.

# THE LIFE
# THAT I HAVE

LEO MARKS
*Violette Szabo's code-poem*

The life that I have
Is all that I have
And the life that I have
Is yours

The love that I have
Of the life that I have
Is yours and yours and yours

A sleep I shall have
A rest I shall have
Yet death will be but a pause

For the peace of my years
In the long green grass
Will be yours and yours and yours

# ITHACA

### C.P. CAVAFY

❖

When you start on your journey to Ithaca,
then pray that the road is long,
full of adventure, full of knowledge.
Do not fear the Lestrygonians
and the Cyclops and the angry Poseidon.
You will never meet such as these on your path,
if your thoughts remain lofty, if a fine
emotion touches your body and your spirit.
You will never meet the Lestrygonians,
the Cyclopes and the fierce Poseidon,
if you do not carry them within your soul,
if your soul does not raise them up before you.

Then pray that the road is long.
That the summer mornings are many,
that you will enter ports seen for the first time
with such pleasure, with such joy!
Stop at Phoenician markets,
and purchase fine merchandise,
mother-of-pearl and corals, amber and ebony,
and pleasurable perfumes of all kinds,
buy as many pleasurable perfumes as you can;
visit hosts of Egyptian cities,

❖

to learn and learn from those who have knowledge.

Always keep Ithaca fixed in your mind.
To arrive there is your ultimate goal.
But do not hurry the voyage at all.
It is better to let it last for long years;
and even to anchor at the isle when you are old,
rich with all that you have gained on the way,
not expecting that Ithaca will offer you riches.

Ithaca has given you the beautiful voyage.
Without her you would never have taken the road.
But she has nothing more to give you.

And if you find her poor, Ithaca has not
    defrauded you.
With the great wisdom you have gained, with so
    much experience,
you must surely have understood by then what
    these Ithacas mean.

# RE-STATEMENT OF ROMANCE

WALLACE STEVENS

The night knows nothing of the chants of night.
It is what it is as I am what I am:
And in perceiving this I best perceive myself

And you. Only we two may interchange
Each in the other what each has to give.
Only we two are one, not you and night,

Nor night and I, but you and I, alone,
So much alone, so deeply by ourselves,
So far beyond the casual solitudes,

That night is only the background of our selves,
Supremely true each to its separate self,
In the pale light that each upon the other throws.

# 'NOW TOUCH THE
AIR SOFTLY'

WILLIAM JAY SMITH

❖

Now touch the air softly,
Step gently. One, two ...
I'll love you till roses
Are robin's-egg blue;
I'll love you till gravel
Is eaten for bread,
And lemons are orange,
And lavender's red.

Now touch the air softly,
Swing gently the broom.
I'll love you till windows
Are all of a room;
And the table is laid,
And the table is bare,
And the ceiling reposes
On bottomless air.

❖

I'll love you till Heaven
Rips the stars from his coat,
And the Moon rows away in
A glass-bottomed boat;
And Orion steps down
Like a diver below,
And Earth is ablaze,
And Ocean aglow.

So touch the air softly,
And swing the broom high.
We will dust the gray mountains,
And sweep the blue sky;
And I'll love you as long
As the furrow the plow,
As However is Ever,
And Ever is Now.

# 'O FAIR! O SWEET! WHEN I DO LOOK ON THEE'

### SIR PHILIP SIDNEY

O fair! O sweet! when I do look on thee,
  In whom all joys so well agree,
Heart and soul do sing in me.
  Just accord all music makes;
In thee just accord excelleth,
Where each part in such peace dwelleth,
  One of other, beauty takes.
Since, then, truth to all minds telleth
  that in thee lives harmony,
  Heart and soul do sing in me.

O fair! O sweet! when I do look on thee,
  In whom all joys so well agree,
Heart and soul do sing in me.
  They that heaven have known do say,
That whoso that grace obtaineth,
To see what fair sight there reigneth,
  Forced are to sing alway:
So then, since that heaven remaineth
  In thy face I plainly see,
  Heart and soul do sing in me.

# THE GATEWAY

## A.D. HOPE

Now the heart sings with all its thousand voices
To hear this city of cells, my body, sing.
The tree through the stiff clay at long last forces
Its thin strong roots and taps the secret spring.

And the sweet waters without intermission
Climb to the tips of its green tenement;
The breasts have borne the grace of their possession,
The lips have felt the pressure of content.

Here I come home: in this expected country
They know my name and speak it with delight.
I am the dream and you my gates of entry,
The means by which I waken into light.

# DAYBREAK

### STEPHEN SPENDER

At dawn she lay with her profile at that angle
Which, when she sleeps, seems the carved face
   of an angel.
Her hair a harp, the hand of a breeze follows
And plays, against the white cloud of the pillows.
Then, in a flush of rose, she woke, and her eyes
   that opened
Swam in blue through her rose flesh that dawned.
From her dew of lips, the drop of one word
Fell like the first of fountains: murmured
'Darling', upon my ears the song of the first bird.
'My dream becomes my dream,' she said, 'come
   true.
I waken from you to my dream of you.'
Oh, my own wakened dream then dared assume
The audacity of her sleep. Our dreams
Poured into each other's arms, like streams.

# FIRST LOVE

## JOHN CLARE

I ne'er was struck before that hour
   With love so sudden and so sweet,
Her face it bloomed like a sweet flower
   And stole my heart away complete.
My face turned pale as deadly pale,
   My legs refused to walk away,
And when she looked, what could I ail?
   My life and all seemed turned to clay.

And then my blood rushed to my face
   And took my eyesight quite away,
The trees and bushes round the place
   Seemed midnight at noonday.
I could not see a single thing,
   Words from my eyes did start—
They spoke as chords do from the string,
   And blood burnt round my heart.

❖

Are flowers the winter's choice?
  Is love's bed always snow?
She seemed to hear my silent voice,
  Not love's appeals to know.
I never saw so sweet a face
  As that I stood before.
My heart has left its dwelling-place
  And can return no more.

# SUMMER STORM

LOUIS SIMPSON

In that so sudden summer storm they tried
Each bed, couch, closet, carpet, car-seat, table,
Both river banks, five fields, a mountain side,
Covering as much ground as they were able.

A lady, coming on them in the dark
In a white fixture, wrote to the newspapers
Complaining of the statues in the park.
By Cupid, but they cut some pretty capers!

The envious oxen in still rings would stand
Ruminating. Their sweet incessant ploughs
I think had changed the contours of the land
And made two modest conies move their house.

God rest them well, and firmly shut the door.
Now they are married Nature breathes once more.

# 'MY MISTRESS' EYES ARE NOTHING LIKE THE SUN'

## William Shakespeare

My mistress' eyes are nothing like the sun;
Coral is far more red than her lips' red:
   If snow be white, why then her breasts are
   dun;
If hairs be wires, black wires grow on her head.
I have seen roses damasked, red and white,
But no such roses see I in her cheeks;
And in some perfumes is there more delight
Than in the breath that from my mistress reeks.
I love to hear her speak; yet well I know
That music hath a far more pleasing sound:
I grant I never saw a goddess go,
My mistress, when she walks, treads on the ground:
   And yet, by heaven, I think my love as rare
   As any she belied with false compare.

# 'SOMEWHERE I HAVE NEVER TRAVELLED, GLADLY BEYOND'

E.E. CUMMINGS

Somewhere i have never travelled,gladly beyond
any experience,your eyes have their silence:
in your most frail gesture are things which enclose me
or which i cannot touch because they are too near

your slightest look easily will unclose me
though i have closed myself as fingers,
you open always petal by petal myself as Spring opens
(touching skilfully,mysteriously)her first rose

or if your wish be to close me,i and
my life will shut very beautifully,suddenly,
as when the heart of this flower imagines
the snow carefully everywhere descending;

❖

nothing which we are to perceive in this world equals
the power of your intense fragility:whose texture
compels me with the colour of its countries,
rendering death and forever with each breathing

(i do not know what it is about you that closes
and opens;only something in me understands
the voice of your eyes is deeper than all roses)
nobody,not even the rain,has such small hands

# THE CASTLE OF THE CORMORANTS

RICHARD BRAUTIGAN

❖

Hamlet with
a cormorant
under his arm
married Ophelia.
She was still
wet from drowning.
She looked like
a white flower
that had been
left in the
rain too long.
I love you,
said Ophelia,
and I love
that dark
bird you
hold in
your arms.

*Big Sur*
*February 1958*

# LOVE'S PHILOSOPHY

### Percy Bysshe Shelley

❖

The fountains mingle with the river
    And the rivers with the Ocean,
The winds of Heaven mix for ever
    With a sweet emotion;
Nothing in the world is single;
    All things by a law divine
In one spirit meet and mingle.
    Why not I with thine?—

See the mountains kiss high Heaven
    And the waves clasp one another;
No sister-flower would be forgiven
    If it disdained its brother;
And the sunlight clasps the earth
    And the moonbeams kiss the sea:
What is all this sweet work worth
    If thou kiss not me?

# RUTH

## THOMAS HOOD

She stood breast high amid the corn,
Clasped by the golden light of morn,
Like the sweetheart of the sun,
Who many a glowing kiss had won.

On her cheek an autumn flush,
Deeply ripened;—such a blush
In the midst of brown was born,
Like red poppies grown with corn.

Round her eyes her tresses fell,
Which were blackest none could tell,
But long lashes veiled a light,
That had else been all too bright.

And her hat, with shady brim,
Made her tressy forehead dim;—
Thus she stood amid the stooks,
Praising God with sweetest looks:—

Sure, I said, heaven did not mean,
Where I reap thou shouldst but glean,
Lay thy sheaf adown and come,
Share my harvest and my home.

# SHE WALKS IN BEAUTY

## GEORGE GORDON, LORD BYRON

She walks in beauty, like the night
  Of cloudless climes and starry skies;
And all that's best of dark and bright
  Meet in her aspect and her eyes:
Thus mellowed to that tender light
  Which heaven to gaudy day denies.

One shade the more, one ray the less,
  Had half impaired the nameless grace
Which waves in every raven tress,
  Or softly lightens o'er her face;
Where thoughts serenely sweet express
  How pure, how dear their dwelling-place.

And on that cheek, and o'er that brow,
  So soft, so calm, yet eloquent,
The smiles that win, the tints that glow,
  But tell of days in goodness spent,
A mind at peace with all below,
  A heart whose love is innocent!

# A DITTY

SIR PHILIP SIDNEY

❖

My true-love hath my heart, and I have his,
　By just exchange one for another given:
I hold his dear, and mine he cannot miss,
　There never was a better bargain driven:
　　My true-love hath my heart, and I have his.

His heart in me keeps him and me in one,
　My heart in him his thoughts and senses guides:
He loves my heart, for once it was his own,
　I cherish his because in me it bides:
　　My true-love hath my heart, and I have his.

# SONG: I HID MY LOVE

## JOHN CLARE

I hid my love when young while I
Couldn't bear the buzzing of a fly;
I hid my love to my despite
Till I could not bear to look at light:
I dare not gaze upon her face
But left her memory in each place;
Where'er I saw a wild flower lie
I kissed and bade my love good-bye.

I met her in the greenest dells,
Where dewdrops pearl the wood bluebells;
The lost breeze kissed her bright blue eye,
The bee kissed and went singing by,
A sunbeam found a passage there,
A gold chain round her neck so fair;
As secret as the wild bee's song
She lay there all the summer long.

❖

I hid my love in field and town
Till e'en the breeze would knock me down;
The Bees seemed singing ballads o'er,
The flyes buzz turned a Lion's roar;
And even silence found a tongue,
To haunt me all the summer long;
The riddle nature could not prove
Was nothing else but secret love.

# 'CARRY HER OVER THE WATER'

W.H. Auden

❖

Carry her over the water,
   And set her down under the tree,
Where the culvers white all day and all night,
   And the winds from every quarter,
Sing agreeably, agreeably, agreeably of love.

Put a gold ring on her finger,
   And press her close to your heart,
While the fish in the lake their snapshots take,
   And the frog, that sanguine singer,
Sings agreeably, agreeably, agreeably of love.

The streets shall all flock to your marriage,
   The houses turn round to look,
The tables and chairs say suitable prayers,
   And the horses drawing your carriage
Sing agreeably, agreeably, agreeably of love.

# THE PASSIONATE SHEPHERD
# TO HIS LOVE

CHRISTOPHER MARLOWE

Come live with me and be my Love,
And we will all the pleasures prove
That valleys, groves, hills, and fields,
Woods, or steepy mountains yields.

And we will sit upon the rocks
Seeing the shepherds feed their flocks,
By shallow rivers, to whose falls
Melodious birds sing madrigals.

And I will make thee beds of roses
And a thousand fragrant posies,
A cap of flowers, and a kirtle
Embroidered all with leaves of myrtle;

A gown made of the finest wool,
Which from our pretty lambs we pull;
Fair linëd slippers for the cold,
With buckles of the purest gold;

❖

A belt of straw and ivy buds
With coral clasps and amber studs;
And if these pleasures may thee move,
Come live with me and be my Love.

The shepherd swains shall dance and sing
For thy delight each May morning:
If these delights thy mind may move,
Then live with me and be my Love.

# A DEDICATION TO MY WIFE

## T.S. ELIOT

❖

To whom I owe the leaping delight
That quickens my senses in our wakingtime
And the rhythm that governs the repose of our
    sleepingtime,
        The breathing in unison

Of lovers whose bodies smell of each other
Who think the same thoughts without need of
    speech
And babble the same speech without need of
    meaning.

No peevish winter wind shall chill
No sullen tropic sun shall wither
The roses in the rose-garden which is ours and
    ours only

But this dedication is for others to read:
These are private words addressed to you in
    public.

# TO CLORIS

Sir Charles Sedley

❖

Cloris, I cannot say your eyes
Did my unwary heart surprise;
Nor will I swear it was your face,
Your shape, or any nameless grace:
For you are so entirely fair,
To love a part, injustice were;
No drowning man can know which drop
Of water his last breath did stop;
So when the stars in heaven appear,
And join to make the night look clear;
The light we no one's bounty call,
But the obliging gift of all.
He that does lips or hands adore,
Deserves them only, and no more;
But I love all, and every part,
And nothing less can ease my heart.
Cupid, that lover, weakly strikes,
Who can express what 'tis he likes.

# SO WHAT IS LOVE?

ANONYMOUS
*Translated by Maria Lovell*

❖

So what is love? If thou wouldst know
The heart alone can tell:
Two minds with but a single thought,
Two hearts that beat as one.

And whence comes Love? Like morning bright
Love comes without thy call.
And how dies Love? A spirit bright,
Love never dies at all.

# THE SONNET

### Elizabeth Barrett Browning

❖

If thou must love me, let it be for naught
   Except for love's sake. Do not say
    'I love her for her smile ... her look ... her
      way
Of speaking gently, ... for a trick of thought
That falls in well with mine, and certes brought
   A sense of pleasant ease on such a day'—
   For these things in themselves, Beloved, may
Be changed, or change for thee,—and love, so
   wrought,
May be unwrought so. Neither love me for
   Thine own dear pity's wiping my cheeks dry,—
A creature might forget to weep, who bore
   Thy comfort long, and lose thy love thereby!
But love me for love's sake, that evermore
   Thou mayst love on, through love's eternity.

# LOVE'S OMNIPRESENCE

J. SYLVESTER

❖

Were I as base as is the lowly plain,
  And you, my Love, as high as heaven above,
Yet should the thoughts of me your humble swain
  Ascend to heaven, in honour of my Love.

Were I as high as heaven above the plain,
  And you, my Love, as humble and as low
As are the deepest bottoms of the main,
  Whereso'er you were, with you my love
    should go.

Were you the earth, dear Love, and I the skies,
  My love should shine on you like to the sun,
And look upon you with ten thousand eyes
  Till heaven wax'd blind, and till the world
    were donè.

Whereso'er I am, below, or else above you,
Whereso'er you are, my heart shall truly love you.

# THE GOOD MORROW

### JOHN DONNE

❖

I wonder by my troth, what thou and I
Did, till we loved? were we not weaned till then?
But sucked on country pleasures, childishly?
Or snorted we i'the seven sleepers' den?
'Twas so; But this, all pleasures fancies be.
If ever any beauty I did see,
Which I desired, and got, 'twas but a dream of thee.

And now good morrow to our waking souls,
Which watch not one another out of fear;
For love, all love of other sights controls,
And makes one little room, an everywhere.
Let sea-discoverers to new worlds have gone,
Let maps to others, worlds on worlds have shown,
Let us possess our world, each hath one, and is one.

❖

My face in thine eye, thine in mine appears,
And true plain hearts do in the faces rest,
Where can we find two better hemispheres
Without sharp North, without declining West?
Whatever dies, was not mixed equally;
If our two loves be one, or, thou and I
Love so alike, that none do slacken, none can die.

# THE FIRST DAY

### CHRISTINA ROSSETTI

I wish I could remember the first day,
First hour, first moment of your meeting me;
If bright or dim the season, it might be
Summer or winter for aught I can say.
So unrecorded did it slip away,
So blind was I to see and to foresee,
So dull to mark the budding of my tree
That would not blossom yet for many a May.
If only I could recollect it! Such
A day of days! I let it come and go
As traceless as a thaw of bygone snow.
It seemed to mean so little, meant so much!
If only now I could recall that touch,
First touch of hand in hand!—Did one but know!

# TO HIS LOVE

WILLIAM SHAKESPEARE

❖

Shall I compare thee to a summer's day?
Thou art more lovely and more temperate:
Rough winds do shake the darling buds of May,
And summer's lease hath all too short a date;

Sometime too hot the eye of heaven shines,
And often is his gold complexion dimm'd:
And every fair from fair sometime declines,
By chance, or nature's changing course, untrimm'd.

But thy eternal summer shall not fade
Nor lose possession of that fair thou owest;
Nor shall death brag thou wanderest in his shade,
When in eternal lines to time thou growest;

So long as men can breathe, or eyes can see,
So long lives this, and this gives life to thee.

# 'LOVE IS MORE THICKER THAN FORGET'

### E.E. CUMMINGS

love is more thicker than forget
more thinner than recall
more seldom than a wave is wet
more frequent than to fail

it is most mad and moonly
and less it shall unbe
than all the sea which only
is deeper than the sea

love is less always than to win
less never than alive
less bigger than the least begin
less littler than forgive

it is most sane and sunly
and more it cannot die
than all the sky which only
is higher than the sky

# FROM 'EPITHALAMION'

Edmund Spenser

Now al is done; bring home the bride againe,
Bring home the triumph of our victory,
Bring home with you the glory of her gaine,
With joyance bring her and with jollity.
Never had man more joyfull day then this,
Whom heaven would heape with blis.
Make feast therefore now all this live long day,
This day for ever to me holy is,
Poure out the wine without restraint or stay,
Poure not by cups, but by the belly full,
Poure out to all that wull,
And sprinkle all the postes and wals with wine,
That they may sweat, and drunken be withall.
Crowne ye God Bacchus with a coronall,
And Hymen also crowne with wreathes of vine,
And let the Graces daunce unto the rest;
For they can doo it best:
The whiles the maydens doe theyr carroll sing,
To which the woods shal answer and theyr eccho ring

# SUDDEN LIGHT

### DANTE GABRIEL ROSSETTI

I have been here before,
  But when or how I cannot tell:
I know the grass beyond the door,
  The sweet keen smell,
The sighing sound, the lights around the shore.

You have been mine before,—
  How long ago I may not know
But just when at that swallow's soar
  Your neck turned so,
Some veil did fall,—I knew it all of yore.

Has this been thus before?
  And shall not thus time's eddying flight
Still with our lives our love restore
  In death's despite,
And day and night yield one delight once more?

# 'I'LL GIVE MY LOVE AN APPLE WITHOUT A CORE'

Anonymous

❖

I'll give my love an apple without a core,
I'll give my love a house without a door,
I'll give my love a palace wherein she may be,
And she may unlock it without any key.

My head is the apple without a core,
My mind is the house without a door,
My heart is the palace wherein she may be,
And she may unlock it without any key.

# SONG

### JOHN FLETCHER

Do not fear to put thy feet
Naked in the river sweet;
Think not leech, or newt, or toad
Will bite thy foot, when thou hast trod:
Nor let the water rising high
As thou wad'st in, make thee cry
And sob; but ever live with me
And not a wave shall trouble thee.

# WE TWO, HOW LONG WE WERE FOOL'D

## WALT WHITMAN

We two, how long we were fool'd,
Now transmuted, we swiftly escape as Nature
 escapes,
We are Nature, long have we been absent, but
 now we return,
We become plants, trunks, foliage, roots, bark,
We are bedded in the ground, we are rocks,
We are oaks, we grow in the openings side by
 side,
We browse, we are two among the wild herds
 spontaneous as any,
We are two fishes swimming in the sea
 together,
We are what locust blossoms are, we drop scent
 around lanes mornings and evenings,
We are also the coarse smut of beasts,
 vegetables, minerals,
We are two predatory hawks, we soar above
 and look down,

❖

We are two resplendent suns, we it is who
    balance ourselves orbic and stellar, we are as
    two comets,
We prowl fang'd and four-footed in the woods,
    we spring on prey,
We are two clouds forenoons and afternoons
    driving overhead,
We are seas mingling, we are two of those
    cheerful waves rolling over each other and
    interwetting each other,
We are what the atmosphere is, transparent,
    receptive, pervious, impervious,
We are snow, rain, cold, darkness, we are each
    product and influence of the globe,
We have circled and circled till we have arrived
    home again, we two,
We have voided all but freedom and all but our
    own joy.

# SONNET XLIII, FROM THE PORTUGUESE

Elizabeth Barrett Browning

How do I love thee? Let me count the ways.
I love thee to the depth and breadth and height
My soul can reach, when feeling out of sight
For the ends of Being and ideal Grace.
I love thee to the level of every day's
Most quiet need, by sun and candlelight.
I love thee freely, as men strive for Right;
I love thee purely, as they turn from Praise.
I love thee with the passion put to use
In my old griefs, and with my childhood's faith.
I love thee with a love I seemed to lose
With my lost saints,—I love thee with the breath,
Smiles, tears, of all my life!—and, if God choose,
I shall but love thee better after death.

# 'WHEN, IN DISGRACE WITH FORTUNE AND MEN'S EYES'

### WILLIAM SHAKESPEARE

When, in disgrace with fortune and men's eyes,
I all alone beweep my outcast state,
And trouble deaf heaven with my bootless' cries,
And look upon myself, and curse my fate,
Wishing me like to one more rich in hope,
Featured like him, like him with friends possessed,
Desiring this man's art, and that man's scope,
With what I most enjoy contented least;
Yet in these thoughts myself almost despising,
Haply I think on thee, and then my state,
Like to the lark at break of day arising
From sullen earth, sings hymns at heaven's gate;
For thy sweet love remembered such wealth brings
That then I scorn to change my state with kings.

# ANONYMOUS FRONTIER GUARD

ANONYMOUS
*Translated from the eighth-century Japanese by*
*Geoffrey Bownas and Anthony Thwaite*

❖

While the leaves of the bamboo rustle
On a cold and frosty night,
The seven layers of clobber I wear
Are not so warm, not so warm
As the body of my wife.

# *AND A*
# Funeral

# 'STOP ALL THE CLOCKS, CUT OFF THE TELEPHONE'

W.H. AUDEN

Stop all the clocks, cut off the telephone,
Prevent the dog from barking with a juicy bone,
Silence the pianos and with muffled drum
Bring out the coffin, let the mourners come.

Let aeroplanes circle moaning overhead
Scribbling on the sky the message He Is Dead,
Put the crêpe bows round the white necks of
   the public doves,
Let the traffic policemen wear black cotton gloves.

He was my North, my South, my East and
   West,
My working week and my Sunday rest,
My noon, my midnight, my talk, my song;
I thought that love would last for ever: I was wrong.

*AND* A Funeral

❖

The stars are not wanted now: put out every one;
Pack up the moon and dismantle the sun;
Pour away the ocean and sweep up the wood.
For nothing now can ever come to any good.

# SHROUD

George Mackay Brown

❖

Seven threads make the shroud,
The white thread,
A green corn thread,
A blue fish thread,
A red stitch, rut and rieving and wrath,
A gray thread
(All winter failing hand falleth on wheel)
The black thread,
And a thread too bright for the eye.

# DUTY

ELLEN S. HOOPER

❖

I slept and dreamed that life was Beauty:
I woke and found that life was Duty:
Was then the dream a shadowy lie?
Toil on, sad heart, courageously,
And thou shalt find thy dream to be
A noonday light and truth to thee.

# 'PENSIVE, ON HER DEAD GAZING, I HEARD THE MOTHER OF ALL'

### WALT WHITMAN

Pensive, on her dead gazing, I heard the Mother of All,
Desperate, on the torn bodies, on the forms covering the battle-fields gazing;
(As the last gun ceased—but the scent of the powder-smoke linger'd;)
As she call'd to her earth with mournful voice while she stalk'd:
Absorb them well, O my earth, she cried—I charge you, lose not my sons! lose not an atom;
And you streams, absorb them well, taking their dear blood;
And you local spots, and you airs that swim above lightly,
And all you essences of soil and growth—and you, my rivers' depths;
And you, mountain sides—and the woods where my dear children's blood, trickling, redden'd;

71

❖

And you trees, down in your roots, to bequeath
    to all future trees,
My dead absorb——my young men's beautiful
    bodies absorb——and their precious, precious,
    precious blood;
Which holding in trust for me, faithfully back
    again give me many a year hence,
In unseen essence and odor of surface and grass,
    centuries hence;
In blowing airs from the fields, back again give
    me my darlings——give my immortal heroes;
Exhale me them centuries hence——breathe me
    their breath——let not an atom be lost;
O years and graves! O air and soil! O my dead,
    an aroma sweet!
Exhale them perennial, sweet death, years,
    centuries hence.

# ON THE BEACH AT
# FONTANA

### JAMES JOYCE

Wind whines and whines the shingle,
The crazy pierstakes groan;
A senile sea numbers each single
Slimesilvered stone.

From whining wind and colder
Grey sea I wrap him warm
And touch his trembling fineboned shoulder
And boyish arm.

Around us fear, descending
Darkness of fear above
And in my heart how deep unending
Ache of love!

# ON MY FIRST SONNE

### BEN JONSON

Farewell, thou child of my right hand, and joy;
My sinne was too much hope of thee, lov'd boy,
Seven yeeres tho'wert lent to me, and I thee pay,
Exacted by thy fate, on the just day.
O, could I loose all father, now. For why
Will man lament the state he should envie?
To have so soone scap'd worlds, and fleshes rage,
And, if no other miserie, yet age?
Rest in soft peace, and, ask'd, say here doth lye
Ben Jonson his best piece of poetrie.
For whose sake, hence-forth, all his bowes be such,
As what he loves may never like too much.

# PAIN

ANONYMOUS

❖

The cry of man's anguish went up to God,
'Lord, take away pain!
The shadow that darkens the world Thou hast made;
The close coiling chain
That strangles the heart: the burden that weighs
On the wings that would soar—
Lord, take away pain from the world Thou hast made
That it love Thee the more!'

Then answered the Lord to the cry of the world,
'Shall I take away pain,
And with it the power of the soul to endure,
Made strong by the strain?
Shall I take away pity that knits heart to heart,
And sacrifice high?
Will ye lose all your heroes that lift from the fire

❖

White brows to the sky?
Shall I take away love that redeems with a price,
And smiles with its loss?
Can ye spare from your lives that would cling
    unto mine
The Christ on his cross?'

# THE NORTH SHIP

PHILIP LARKIN
*Legend*

I saw three ships go sailing by,
Over the sea, the lifting sea,
And the wind rose in the morning sky,
And one was rigged for a long journey.

The first ship turned towards the west,
Over the sea, the running sea,
And by the wind was all possessed
And carried to a rich country.

The second turned towards the east,
Over the sea, the quaking sea,
And the wind hunted it like a beast
To anchor in captivity.

The third ship drove towards the north,
Over the sea, the darkening sea,
But no breath of wind came forth,
And the decks shone frostily.

❖

The northern sky rose high and black
Over the proud unfruitful sea,
East and west the ships came back
Happily or unhappily:

But the third went wide and far
Into an unforgiving sea
Under a fire-spilling star,
And it was rigged for a long journey.

# 'THE LOWEST TREES HAVE TOPS, THE ANT HER GALL'

Sir Edward Dyer

Where waters smoothest run, there deepest are
   the fords;
The dial stirs, yet none perceives it move;
The firmest faith is found in fewest words;
The turtles do not sing, and yet they love;
   True hearts have ears and eyes, no tongues to
     speak:
   They hear and see, and sigh, and then they
     break.

# 'DO NOT GO GENTLE INTO THAT GOOD NIGHT'

### Dylan Thomas

Do not go gentle into that good night,
Old age should burn and rave at close of day;
Rage, rage against the dying of the light.

Though wise men at their end know dark is right,
Because their words had forked no lightning they
Do not go gentle into that good night.

Good men, the last wave by, crying how bright
Their frail deeds might have danced in a green bay,
Rage, rage against the dying of the light.

Wild men who caught and sang the sun in flight,
And learn, too late, they grieved it on its way,
Do not go gentle into that good night.

❖

Grave men, near death, who see with blinding sight
Blind eyes could blaze like meteors and be gay,
Rage, rage against the dying of the light.

And you, my father, there on the sad height,
Curse, bless, me now with your fierce tears, I pray.
Do not go gentle into that good night.
Rage, rage against the dying of the light.

# IN THE DAYS WHEN WE ARE DEAD

Henry Lawson

❖

Listen! The end draws nearer,
Nearer the morning—or night—
And I see with a vision clearer
That the beginning was right!
These shall be words to remember
When all has been done and said,
And my fame is a dying ember
In the days when I am dead.

Listen! We wrote in sorrow,
And we wrote by candle light;
We took no heed of the morrow,
And I think that we were right—
(*To-morrow*, but not the day after,
And I think that we were right).

We wrote of a world that was human
And we wrote of a blood that was red,
For a child, or a man, or a woman—
Remember when we are dead.

❖

Listen! We wrote not for money,
And listen! We wrote not for fame—
We wrote for the milk and the honey
Of Kindness, and not for a name.

We paused not, nor faltered for any,
Though many fell back where we led;
We wrote of the few for the many—
*Remember when we are dead.*

We suffered as few men suffer,
Yet laugh as few men laugh;
We grin as the road grows rougher,
And a bitterer cup we quaff.

We lived for Right and for Laughter,
And we fought for a Nation ahead—
Remember it, friends, hereafter,
In the years when I am dead—
For to-morrow and not the day after,
For ourselves, and a Nation ahead.

# CROSSING THE BAR

ALFRED, LORD TENNYSON

❖

Sunset and evening star,
   And one clear call for me!
And may there be no moaning of the bar,
   When I put out to sea,

But such a tide as moving seems asleep,
   Too full for sound and foam,
When that which drew from out the boundless de
   Turns again home.

Twilight and evening bell,
   And after that the dark!
And may there be no sadness of farewell,
   When I embark;

For tho' from out our bourne of Time and Place
   The flood may bear me far,
I hope to see my Pilot face to face
   When I have crost the bar.

# THE DEAD

Rupert Brooke

❖

These hearts were woven of human joys and
   cares,
Washed marvellously with sorrow, swift to
   mirth.
The years had given them kindness. Dawn was
   theirs,
And sunset, and the colours of the earth.
These had seen movement, and heard music;
   known
Slumber and waking; loved; gone proudly
   friended;
Felt the quick stir of wonder; sat alone;
Touched flowers and furs and cheeks. All this is
   ended.

There are waters blown by changing winds to
   laughter
And lit by the rich skies, all day. And after,
Frost, with a gesture, stays the waves that dance
And wandering loveliness. He leaves a white
Unbroken glory, a gathered radiance,
A width, a shining peace, under the night.

# I THINK CONTINUALLY OF THOSE WHO WERE TRULY GREAT

STEPHEN SPENDER

I think continually of those who were truly great.
Who, from the womb, remembered the soul's
  history
Through corridors of light where the hours are suns
Endless and singing. Whose lovely ambition
Was that their lips, still touched with fire,
Should tell of the Spirit clothed from head to
  foot in song.
And who hoarded from the Spring branches
The desires falling across their bodies like blossoms.

What is precious is never to forget
The essential delight of the blood drawn from
  ageless springs
Breaking through rocks in worlds before our earth.

❖

Never to deny its pleasure in the morning simple light
Nor its grave evening demand for love.
Never to allow gradually the traffic to smother
With noise and fog the flowering of the spirit.

Near the snow, near the sun, in the highest fields
See how these names are fêted by the waving grass
And by the streamers of white cloud
And whispers of wind in the listening sky.
The names of those who in their lives fought for life
Who wore at their hearts the fire's centre.
Born of the sun they travelled a short while towards
   the sun,
And left the vivid air signed with their honour.

# DEATH BE NOT PROUD

### John Donne

Death be not proud, though some have called thee
Mighty and dreadful, for, thou art not so,
For, those whom you think'st thou dost overthrow
Die not, poor Death, nor yet canst thou kill me.
From rest and sleep, which but thy pictures be,
Much pleasure, then from thee much more must
    flow,
And soonest our best men with thee do go
Rest of their bones, and souls' delivery!
Thou art slave to Fate, chance, kings, and
    desperate men,
And dost with poison, war, and sickness dwell,
And poppy, or charms can make us sleep as well,
And better than thy stroke. Why swell's thou then?
One short sleep past, we wake eternally,
And Death shall be no more: Death, thou shalt
    die.

# THE VAGABOND

ROBERT LOUIS STEVENSON
*To an Air of Schubert*

❖

Give to me the life I love,
  Let the lave go by me,
Give the jolly heaven above
  And the byway nigh me.
Bed in the bush with stars to see,
  Bread I dip in the river—
There's the life for a man like me,
  There's the life for ever.

Let the blow fall soon or late,
  Let what will be o'er me;
Give the face of earth around
  And the road before me.
Wealth I seek not, hope nor love,
  Nor a friend to know me;
All I seek, the heaven above
  And the road below me.

❖

Or let autumn fall on me
    Where afield I linger,
Silencing the bird on tree,
    Biting the blue finger.
White as meal the frosty field—
    Warm the fireside haven—
Not to autumn will I yield,
    Not to winter even!

Let the blow fall soon or late,
    Let what will be o'er me;
Give the face of earth around,
    And the road before me.
Wealth I ask not, hope nor love,
    Nor a friend to know me;
All I ask, the heaven above
    And the road below me.

# ADIEU! AND AU REVOIR

John Oxenham

❖

As you love me, let there be
No mourning when I go,—
No tearful eyes,
No hopeless sighs,
No woe,—nor even sadness!
Indeed I would not have you sad,
For I myself shall be full glad,
With the high triumphant gladness
Of a soul made free
Of God's sweet liberty.
—No windows darkened;

For my own
Will be flung wide as ne'er before,
To catch the radiant inpour
Of Love that shall in full atone
For all the ills that I have done;
And the good things left undone;
—No voices hushed;
My own, full flushed
With an immortal hope, will rise
In ecstasies of new-born bliss
And joyful melodies.

*AND* A Funeral

❖

Rather, of your sweet courtesy,
Rejoice with me
At my soul's loosing from captivity.
Wish me 'Bon Voyage!'
As you do a friend
Whose joyous visit finds its happy end.
And bid me both 'à Dieu!'
And 'au revoir!'
Since, though I come no more,
I shall be waiting there to greet you,
At His Door.

And, as the feet of The Bearers tread
The ways I trod,
Think not of me as dead,
But rather—
'Happy, thrice happy, he whose course is sped!
He has gone home—to God,
His Father!'

# ON ALL SOULS' DAY

CHARLES CAUSLEY

Last night they lit your glass with wine
And brought for you the sweet soul-cake,
And blessed the room with candle-shine
For the grave journey you would make.

They told me not to stir between
The midnight strokes of one and two,
And I should see you come again
To view the scene that once you knew.

'Good night,' they said, and journeyed on.
I turned the key, and—turning—smiled,
And in the quiet house alone
I slept serenely as a child.

Innocent was that sleep, and free,
And when the first of morning shone
I had no need to gaze and see
If crumb, or bead of wine, had gone.

❖

My heart was easy as this bloom
Of waters rising by the bay.
I did not watch where you might come,
For you had never been away.
For you have never been away.

# EVEN SUCH IS TIME

Sir Walter Raleigh

❖

Even such is time, which takes in trust
Our youth, our joys, and all we have,
And pays us but with age and dust;
Who, in the dark and silent grave,
When we have wandered all our ways,
Shuts up the story of our days,
And from which earth and grave and dust,
The Lord shall raise me up, I trust.

# LADY HEGURI

ANONYMOUS
*Translated from the Japanese by*
*Geoffrey Bownas and Anthony Thwaite*

❖

A thousand years, you said,
as our hearts melted.
I look at the hand you held,
and the ache is hard to bear.

# ELEGY FOR HIMSELF

CHIDIOCK TICHBORNE
*Written in the Tower before his execution, 1586*

❖

My prime of youth is but a frost of cares;
  My feast of joy is but a dish of pain;
My crop of corn is but a field of tares;
  And all my good is but vain hope of gain:
The day is past, and yet I saw no sun;
And now I live, and now my life is done.

My tale was heard, and yet it was not told;
  My fruit is fall'n, and yet my leaves are
    green;
My youth is spent, and yet I am not old;
  I saw the world, and yet I was not seen:
My thread is cut, and yet it is not spun;
And now I live, and now my life is done.

I sought my death, and found it in my womb;
  I looked for life, and saw it was a shade;
I trod the earth, and knew it was my tomb;
  And now I die, and now I was but made;
My glass is full, and now my glass is run;
And now I live, and now my life is done.

# THE DARKLING THRUSH

### Thomas Hardy

I leant upon a coppice gate
  When Frost was spectre-gray,
And Winter's dregs made desolate
  The weakening eye of day.
The tangled bine-stems scored the sky
  Like strings of broken lyres,
And all mankind that haunted nigh
  Had sought their household fires.

The land's sharp features seemed to be
  The Century's corpse outleant,
His crypt the cloudy canopy,
  The wind his death-lament.
The ancient pulse of germ and birth
  Was shrunken hard and dry,
And every spirit upon earth
  Seemed fervourless as I.

❖

At once a voice arose among
  The bleak twigs overhead
In a full-hearted evensong
  Of joy illimited;
An aged thrush, frail, gaunt, and small,
  In blast-beruffled plume,
Had chosen thus to fling his soul
  Upon the growing gloom.

So little cause for carolings
  Of such ecstatic sound
Was written on terrestrial things
  Afar or nigh around,
That I could think there trembled through
  His happy goodnight air
Some blessed Hope, whereof he knew
  And I was unaware.

# INDIAN PRAYER

ANONYMOUS
*Traditional*

❖

When I am dead
Cry for me a little
Think of me sometimes
But not too much.
Think of me now and again
As I was in life
At some moments it's pleasant to recall
But not for long.
Leave me in peace
And I shall leave you in peace
And while you live
Let your thoughts be with the living.

# 'BREAK, BREAK, BREAK'

ALFRED, LORD TENNYSON

❖

Break, break, break,
  On thy cold gray stones, O Sea!
And I would that my tongue could utter
  The thoughts that arise in me.

O well for the fisherman's boy,
  That he shouts with his sister at play!
O well for the sailor lad,
  That he sings in his boat on the bay!

And the stately ships go on
  To their haven under the hill;
But O for the touch of a vanish'd hand,
  And the sound of a voice that is still!

Break, break, break
  At the foot of thy crags, O Sea!
But the tender grace of a day that is dead
  Will never come back to me.

# 'AND DEATH SHALL HAVE NO DOMINION'

DYLAN THOMAS

And death shall have no dominion.
Dead men naked they shall be one
With the man in the wind and the west moon;
When their bones are picked clean and the clean
   bones gone,
They shall have stars at elbow and foot;
Though they go mad they shall be sane,
Though they sink through the sea they shall rise
   again;
Though lovers be lost love shall not;
And death shall have no dominion.

And death shall have no dominion.
Under the windings of the sea
They lying long shall not die windily;
Twisting on racks when sinews give way,
Strapped to a wheel, yet they shall not break;
Faith in their hands shall snap in two,
And the unicorn evils run them through;
Split all ends up they shan't crack;
And death shall have no dominion.

❖

And death shall have no dominion.
No more may gulls cry at their ears
Or waves break loud on the seashores;
Where blew a flower may a flower no more
Lift its head to the blows of the rain;
Though they be mad and dead as nails,
Heads of the characters hammer through daisies;
Break in the sun till the sun breaks down,
And death shall have no dominion.

# DIRGE WITHOUT MUSIC

EDNA ST VINCENT MILLAY

❖

I am not resigned to the shutting away of loving
   hearts in the hard ground
So it is, and so it will be, for so it has been,
   time out of mind:
Into the darkness they go, the wise and the
   lovely. Crowned
With lilies and with laurel they go: but I am not
   resigned.

Lovers and thinkers, into the earth with you.
Be one with the dull, the indiscriminate dust.
A fragment of what you felt, of what you knew,
A formula, a phrase remains—but the best is lost.

The answers quick and keen, the honest look,
   the laughter, the love—
They are gone. They have gone to feed the
   roses. Elegant and curled
It's the blossom. Fragrant is the blossom. I
   know. But I do not approve.
More precious was the light in your eyes than all
   the roses in the world.

❖

Down, down, down into the darkness of the
  grave
Gently they go, the beautiful, the tender, the
  kind:
Quietly they go, the intelligent, the witty, the
  brave.
I know. But I do not approve. And I am not
  resigned.

# 1/THE CURVE OF
# FORGOTTEN THINGS

RICHARD BRAUTIGAN

❖

Things slowly curve out of sight
until they are gone. Afterwards
    only the curve
    remains.

# FAREWELL

## ANNE BRONTË

❖

Farewell to Thee! But not farewell
To all my fondest thoughts of Thee;
Within my heart they still shall dwell
And they shall cheer and comfort me.

Life seems more sweet that Thou didst live
And men more true that Thou wert one;
Nothing is lost that Thou didst give,
Nothing destroyed that Thou hast done.

# WALKING AWAY

## C. Day Lewis

❖

It is eighteen years ago, almost to the day—
A sunny day with the leaves just turning,
The touch-lines new-ruled—since I watched you play
Your first game of football, then, like a satellite
Wrenched from its orbit, go drifting away

Behind a scatter of boys. I can see
You walking away from me towards the school
With the pathos of a half-fledged thing set free
Into a wilderness, the gait of one
Who finds no path where the path should be.

That hesitant figure, eddying away
Like a winged seed loosened from its parent stem,
Has something I never quite grasp to convey
About nature's give-and-take—the small, the scorching
Ordeals which fire one's irresolute clay.

❖

I have had worse partings, but none that so
Gnaws at my mind still. Perhaps it is roughly
Saying what God alone could perfectly show—
How selfhood begins with a walking away,
And love is proved in the letting go.

# ULYSSES

ALFRED, LORD TENNYSON

It little profits that an idle king,
By this still hearth, among these barren crags,
Matched with an aged wife, I mete and dole
Unequal laws unto a savage race,
That hoard, and sleep, and feed, and know not me.
I cannot rest from travel; I will drink
Life to the lees. All times I have enjoyed
Greatly, have suffered greatly, both with those
That loved me, and alone; on shore, and when
Through scudding drifts the rainy Hyades
Vexed the dim sea. I am become a name;
For always roaming with a hungry heart
Much have I seen and known,—cities of men
And manners, climates, councils, governments,
Myself not least, but honored of them all;
And drunk delight of battle with my peers,
Far on the ringing plains of windy Troy.
I am a part of all that I have met;
Yet all experience is an arch wherethrough
Gleams that untraveled world whose margin fade
For ever and for ever when I move.
How dull it is to pause, to make an end,

❖

To rest unburnished, not to shine in use,
As though to breathe were life. Life piled on life
Were all too little, and of one to me
Little remains; but every hour is saved
From that eternal silence, something more,
A bringer of new things; and vile it were
For some three suns to store and hoard myself,
And this gray spirit yearning in desire
To follow knowledge like a sinking star,
Beyond the utmost bound of human thought.
　　This is my son, mine own Telemachus,
To whom I leave the scepter and the isle—
Well-loved of me, discerning to fulfill
This labor, by slow prudence to make mild
A rugged people, and through soft degrees
Subdue them to the useful and the good.
Most blameless is he, centered in the sphere
Of common duties, decent not to fail
In offices of tenderness, and pay
Meet adoration to my household gods,
When I am gone. He works his work, I mine.
　　There lies the port; the vessel puffs her sail;
There gloom the dark, broad seas. My mariners,

111

❖

Souls that have toiled, and wrought, and thought
    with me—
That ever with a frolic welcome took
The thunder and the sunshine, and opposed
Free hearts, free foreheads—you and I are old;
Old age hath yet his honor and his toil;
Death closes all—but something ere the end,
Some work of noble note, may yet be done
Not unbecoming men that strove with Gods.
The lights begin to twinkle from the rocks;
The long day wanes; the slow moon climbs; the deep
Moans round with many voices. Come, my friends,
'Tis not too late to seek a newer world.
Push off, and sitting well in order smite
The sounding furrows; for my purpose holds
To sail beyond the sunset, and the baths
Of all the western stars, until I die.
It may be that the gulfs will wash us down:
It may be we shall touch the Happy Isles
And see the great Achilles, whom we knew.
Though much is taken, much abides; and though

❖

We are not now that strength which in old days
Moved earth and heaven, that which we are, we are,
One equal temper of heroic hearts,
Made weak by time and fate, but strong in will
To strive, to seek, to find, and not to yield.

# THE OLD MEN ADMIRING THEMSELVES IN THE WATER

W.B. YEATS

I heard the old, old men say,
'Everything alters,
And one by one we drop away.'
They had hands like claws, and their knees
Were twisted like the old thorn trees
By the waters.
I heard the old, old men say,
'All that's beautiful drifts away
Like the waters.'

# THE SINGLE HERO

Mark van Doren

❖

This man kept courage when the map of fear
Was continents, was paleness to the poles,
Was Jupiter milk white, was Venus burning.
The very stones lay liquid with despair,
And the firm earth was bottomless. This man

Could walk upon that water; nay, he stamped
Till the drops gravelled, till a sound returned
Of pillars underheel, of granite growing.
This man, alone on seas, was not afraid.
So continents came back. So color widened:

Bands upon blankness. So the other men,
The millions, lifted feet and let them down;
And the soil held. So courage's cartographer,
Having his globe again, restored each mass,
Each meadow. And the grasshoppers sang to him.

# CLOUDS

RUPERT BROOKE

❖

Down the blue night the unending columns press
In noiseless tumult, break and wave and flow,
    Now 'tread the far South, or lift rounds of snow
Up to the white moon's hidden loveliness.
Some pause in their grave wandering comradeless,
    And now with profound gesture vague and slow,
    As who would pray good for the world, but know
Their benediction empty as they bless.

They say the Dead die not, but remain
    Near to the rich heirs of their grief and mirth.
    I think they ride the calm mid-heaven, as these,
In wise majestic melancholy train,
    And watch the moon, and the still-raging seas,
And men, coming and going on the earth.

# 'BECAUSE I COULD NOT STOP FOR DEATH'

EMILY DICKINSON

Because I could not stop for Death–
He kindly stopped for me–
The Carriage held but just Ourselves–
And Immortality.

We slowly drove–He knew no haste
And I had put away
My labor and my leisure too,
For His Civility–

We passed the School, where Children strove
At Recess–in the Ring–
We passed the Fields of Gazing Grain–
We passed the Setting Sun–

Or rather–He passed Us–
The Dews drew quivering and chill–
For only Gossamer, my Gown–
My Tippet–only Tulle–

*AND* A Funeral

We paused before a House that seemed
A Swelling of the Ground—
The Roof was scarcely visible—
The Cornice—in the Ground—

Since then—'tis Centuries—and yet
Feels shorter than the Day
I first surmised the Horses' Heads
Were toward Eternity—

# G.M.B.

Donald Davie
*(10.7.77)*

Old oak, old timber, sunk and rooted
  In the organic cancer
Of Devon soil, the need she had
  You could not answer.

Old wash and wump, the narrow seas
  Mindlessly breaking
She scanned lifelong; and yet the tide
  There's no mistaking

She mistook. She never thought,
  It seems, that the soft thunder
She heard nearby, the pluck and slide,
  Might tow her under.

I have as much to do with the dead
  And the dying, as with the living
Nowadays; and failing them is
  Past forgiving.

*AND* A Funeral

❖

As soon be absolved for that, as if
  A tree, or a sea, should be shriven;
And yet the truth is, fail we must
  And be forgiven.

# IF I COULD TELL YOU

W.H. AUDEN

❖

Time will say nothing but I told you so,
Time only knows the price we have to pay;
If I could tell you I would let you know.

If we should weep when clowns put on their show,
If we should stumble when musicians play,
Time will say nothing but I told you so.

There are no fortunes to be told, although,
Because I love you more than I can say,
If I could tell you I would let you know.

The winds must come from somewhere when
    they blow,
There must be reasons why the leaves decay;
Time will say nothing but I told you so.

Perhaps the roses really want to grow,
The vision seriously intends to stay;
If I could tell you I would let you know.

*AND* A Funeral

❖

Suppose the lions all get up and go,
And all the brooks and soldiers run away;
Will Time say nothing but I told you so?
If I could tell you I would let you know.

# TO A DEAD MAN

### Carl Sandburg

Over the dead line we have called to you
To come across with a word to us,
Some beaten whisper of what happens
Where you are over the dead line
Deaf to our calls and voiceless.

The flickering shadows have not answered
Nor your lips sent a signal
Whether love talks and roses grow
And the sun breaks at morning
Splattering the sea with crimson.

# PROSPICE

ROBERT BROWNING

Fear death?——to feel the fog in my throat,
 The mist in my face,
When the snows begin, and the blasts denote
 I am nearing the place,
The power of the night, the press of the storm,
 The post of the foe;
Where he stands, the Arch Fear in a visible form,
 Yet the strong man must go:
For the journey is done and the summit attained,
 And the barriers fall,
Though a battle's to fight ere the guerdon be
 gained,
 The reward of it all.
I was ever a fighter, so——one fight more,
 The best and the last!
I would hate that death bandaged my eyes, and
 forbore,
 And bade me creep past.
No! let me taste the whole of it, fare like my
 peers
 The heroes of old,

❖

Bear the brunt, in a minute pay glad life's arrears
  Of pain, darkness and cold.
For sudden the worst turns the best to the brave,
  The black minute's at end,
And the elements' rage, the fiend-voices that rave,
  Shall dwindle, shall blend,
Shall change, shall become first a peace out of pain,
  stonThen a light, then thy breast,
O thou soul of my soul! I shall clasp thee again,
  And with God be the rest!

# POEM

## Langston Hughes

❖

I loved my friend.
He went away from me.
There's nothing more to say.
The poem ends,
Soft as it began—
I loved my friend.

# THE GATE OF THE YEAR

M. LOUISE HASKINS

❖

And I said to the man who stood at the gate of
   the year:
'Give me a light, that I may tread safely into the
   unknown!'
And he replied:
'Go out into the darkness and put your hand
   into the Hand of God.
That shall be to you better than light and safer
   than a known way.'
So, I went forth, and finding the Hand of God,
   trod gladly into the night
And He led me toward the hills and the
   breaking of day in the lone East.

So, heart, be still!
What need our little life,
Our human life, to know,
If God hath comprehension?
In all the dizzy strife
Of things both high and low
God hideth His intention.

# ETERNITY

## WILLIAM BLAKE

❖

He who binds to himself a joy
Does the winged life destroy;
But he who kisses the joy as it flies
Lives in eternity's sun rise.

# LET ME NOT SEE OLD AGE

D.R. GERAINT JONES

Let me not see old age: Let me not hear
The proffered help, the mumbled sympathy,
The well-meant tactful sophistries that mock
Pathetic husks who once were strong and free,
And in youth's fickle triumph laughed and sang,
Loved, and were foolish; and at the close have seen
The fruits of folly garnered, and that love,
Tamed and encaged, stale into grey routine.
Let me not see old age; I am content
With my few crowded years; laughter and strength
And song have lit the beacon of my life.
Let me not see it fade, but when the long
September shadows steal across the square,
Grant me this wish; they may not find me there.

# 'SOMETHING HAS SPOKEN
TO ME IN THE NIGHT'

THOMAS WOLFE

Something has spoken to me in the night,
Burning the tapers of the waning year;
Something has spoken in the night,
And told me I shall die, I know not where.

Saying:
'To lose the earth you know, for greater knowing;
To lose the life you have, for greater life;
To leave the friends you loved, for greater loving;
To find a land more kind than home, more large
    than earth—

'Whereon the pillars of this earth are founded,
Toward which the conscience of the world is
    tending—
A wind is rising, and the rivers flow.'

# REMEMBER

CHRISTINA ROSSETTI

❖

Remember me when I am gone away,
　Gone far away into the silent land;
　When you can no more hold me by the hand,
Nor I half turn to go, yet turning stay.
Remember me when no more day by day
　You tell me of our future that you planned
　Only remember me; you understand
It will be late to counsel then or pray.
Yet if you should forget me for a while
　And afterwards remember, do not grieve:
　For if the darkness and corruption leave
　A vestige of the thoughts that once I had,
Better by far you should forget and smile
　Than that you should remember and be sad.

# 'IN BEAUTY MAY I WALK'

Anonymous
*Translated from the Navajo by Jerome K. Rothenberg*

In beauty                                      may I walk
All day long                                   may I walk
Through the returning seasons        may I walk
Beautifully will I possess again
Beautifully birds
Beautifully joyful birds
On the trail marked with pollen       may I walk
With grasshoppers about my feet     may I walk
With dew about my feet                   may I walk
With beauty                                    may I walk
With beauty before me                    may I walk
With beauty behind me                    may I walk
With beauty above me                      may I walk
With beauty all around me               may I walk
In old age, wandering on a trail of beauty
                                          lively,    may I walk
In old age, wandering on a trail of beauty
                                  living again,    may I walk
It is finished in beauty
It is finished in beauty

# THE BURNING OF THE LEAVES

Laurence Binyon

Now is the time for the burning of the leaves.
They go to the fire; the nostril pricks with smoke
Wandering slowly into the weeping mist.
Brittle and blotched, ragged and rotten sheaves!
A flame seizes the smouldering ruin, and bites
On stubborn stalks that crackle as they resist.

The last hollyhock's fallen tower is dust:
All the spices of June are a bitter reek,
All the extravagant riches spent and mean.
All burns! the reddest rose is a ghost.
Sparks whirl up, to expire in the mist: the wild
Fingers of fire are making corruption clean.

❖

Now is the time for stripping the spirit bare,
Time for the burning of days ended and done,
Idle solace of things that have gone before,
Rootless hope and fruitless desire are there:
Let them go to the fire with never a look behind.
That world that was ours is a world that is ours
    no more

They will come again, the leaf and the flower,
    to arise
From squalor of rottenness into the old
    splendour,
And magical scents to a wondering memory
    bring;
The same glory, to shine upon different eyes.
Earth cares for her own ruins, naught for ours.
Nothing is certain, only the certain spring.

# SAY NOT THE STRUGGLE
# NAUGHT AVAILETH

### Arthur Hugh Clough

Say not the struggle naught availeth,
  The labour and the wounds are vain,
The enemy faints not, nor faileth,
  And as things have been, things remain.

If hopes were dupes, fears may be liars;
  It may be, in yon smoke concealed,
Your comrades chase e'en now the fliers,
  And, but for you, possess the field.

For while the tired waves, vainly breaking,
  Seem here no painful inch to gain,
Far back through creeks and inlets making
  Comes silent, flooding in, the main.

And not by eastern windows only,
  When daylight comes, comes in the light;
In front the sun climbs slow, how slowly,
  But westward, look, the land is bright!

# BEYOND THE HEADLINES

### PATRICK KAVANAGH

Then I saw the wild geese flying
In fair formation to their bases in Inchicore
And I knew that these wings would outwear the
    wings of war
And a man's simple thoughts outlive the day's
    loud lying.
Don't fear, don't fear, I said to my soul.
The Bedlam of Time is an empty bucket rattled,
'Tis you who will say in the end who best
    battles.
Only they who fly home to God have flown at all.

# A SONG OF LIVING

AMELIA JOSEPHINE BURR

❖

Because I have loved life, I shall have no sorrow
    to die.
I have sent up my gladness on wings, to be lost
    in the blue of the sky.
I have run and leaped with the rain, I have taken
    the wind to my breast.
My cheek like a drowsy child to the face of the
    earth I have pressed.
Because I have loved life, I shall have no sorrow
    to die.

I have kissed young Love on the lips, I have
    heard his song to the end.
I have struck my hand like a seal in the loyal
    hand of a friend.
I have known the peace of heaven, the comfort
    of work done well.
I have longed for death in the darkness and risen
    alive out of hell.
Because I have loved life, I shall have no sorrow
    to die.

❖

I give a share of my soul to the world where
　my course is run.
I know that another shall finish the task I must
　leave undone.
I know that no flower, nor flint was in vain on
　the path I trod.
As one looks on a face through a window,
　through life I have looked on God.
Because I have loved life, I shall have no sorrow
　to die.

# 'DO NOT STAND AT MY GRAVE AND WEEP'

## ANONYMOUS

❖

Do not stand at my grave and weep,
I am not there, I do not sleep.

I am a thousand winds that blow,
I am the diamond glints on snow,
I am the sunlight and ripened grain.
I am the gentle Autumn rain.
When you awake in the morning hush,
I am the swift upflinging rush
of quiet birds in circling flight.
I am the soft star shine at night.

Do not stand at my grave and cry,
I am not there, I did not die.

# ❖ ACKNOWLEDGEMENTS ❖

**W. H. Auden:** 'If I Could Tell You', 'Carry her over the water' & 'Stop all the clocks, cut off the telephone' from *Collected Poems* by W. H. Auden, Faber and Faber Limited; **Richard Brautigan**: '1/The Curve of Forgotten Things' from *Loading Mercury with a Pitchfork* by Richard Brautigan, copyright © 1971. 'The Castle of the Cormorants' from *The Pill Versus the Springhill Mine Disaster* by Richard Brautigan, copyright © 1968 by Richard Brautigan. Renewal copyright 1996 by Ianthe Brautigan Swensen. Reprinted by permission; **George Mackay Brown**: 'Shroud' from *Fishermen with Ploughs* by George Mackay Brown, John Murray (Publishers) Ltd.; **Charles Causley**: 'On All Souls' Day' from *Collected Poems* by Charles Causley, Macmillan; **C. P. Cavafy**: 'Ithaca' from *The Complete Poems of Cavafy*, copyright © 1961 and renewed 1989 by Rae Dalven, reprinted by permission of Harcourt Brace & Company; **E. E. Cummings**: 'somewhere i have never travelled, gladly beyond', 'love is more thicker than forget' and 'if i have made, mylady, intricate' are reprinted from *Complete Poems 1904–1962* by E. E. Cummings, edited by

George J. Firmage, by permission W. W. Norton &
Company Ltd. Copyright © 1931, 1979, 1991 by
the Trustees for the E. E. Commings Trust and
George James Firmage; **Donald Davie**: 'G. M. B.'
from *Collected Poems* by Donald Davie, Carcanet
Press Limited; **C. Day Lewis**: 'Walking Away'
from *The Gate* by C. Day Lewis reprinted by per-
mission of the Peters Fraser and Dunlop Group
Ltd; **T. S. Eliot**: 'A Dedication To My Wife' from
*Collected Poems 1909–1962* by T. S. Eliot, Faber and
Faber Limited; **A. D. Hope**: 'The Gateway' from
*Selected Poems* by A. D. Hope, HarperCollins
Publishers Australia; **Langston Hughes**: 'Poem',
by permission Harold Ober Assocation; **Patrick
Kavanagh**: 'Beyond the Headlines' by kind per-
mission of the Trustees of the Estate of Patrick
Kavanagh, c/o Peter Fallon, Literary Agent,
Loughcrew, Oldcastle, Co. Meath, Ireland; **Philip
Larkin**: 'The North Ship' from *Collected Poems* by
Philip Larkin, Faber and Faber Limited; **Leo
Marks**: 'The Life that I Have', Big Ben Music Ltd;
**Edna St Vincent Millay**: 'Dirge Without Music'
copyright © The Estate of Edna St Vincent Millay;
**Carl Sandburg**: 'To a Dead Man' from *Chicago*

*Poems* by Carl Sandburg, copyright 1916 by Holt, Rinehart and Winston, Inc. and renewed 1944 by Carl Sandburg, reprinted by permission of Harcourt Brace & Company; **May Sarton**: 'Prothalamion', copyright © The estate of the late May Sarton; **Louis Simpson**: 'Summer Storm' from *A Dream of Governors* © 1955, 1956, 1957, 1959, Wesleyan University Press by permission of University Press of New England; **Stephen Spender**: 'Daybreak', from *Collected Poems 1928–1985* by Stephen Spender, Faber and Faber Limited; 'I Think Continually of Those Who Were Truly Great' from *Collected Poems 1928–1953* by Stephen Spender, copyright © 1934 by The Modern Library, Inc. Copyright © 1930, 1942, 1947, 1952 © 1955 by Stephen Spender. Reprinted by permission of Random House, Inc.; **Kuan Tao-Sheng**: 'Married Love' from *Women Poets of China*. Copyright © 1973 by Kenneth Rexroth and Ling Chung. Reprinted by permission of New Directions Publishing Corp.; **Dylan Thomas**: 'Do not go gentle into that good night' and 'And death shall have no dominion' from *The Poems* by Dylan Thomas, J. M. Dent.

# ❖ INDEX ❖

**Bold type = poet's name**
**Quotation marks = where first line of**
**poem is commonly used as title**

*Writing Camps with John Marsden*

The magnificent Tye Estate, just 25 minutes from Melbourne's Tullamarine Airport, is proud to offer writing camps with John Marsden.

Young people and adults from all over Australia can work closely with John on their writing, as well as having a wonderful time making new friends and enjoying the range of activities on one of Australia's most famous properties.

The Tye Estate offers quality accommodation and excellent meals, with supervision by friendly and experienced staff. Between the workshops with John, you can explore 850 acres of bush, with beautiful creeks and spectacular views. Mountain bikes, horse riding, bushwalking, orienteering, and a picnic at nearby Hanging Rock, are among the highlights of your memorable stay at the Tye Estate.

School camps, holiday camps and adult workshops are available.

For details, write to:  The Tye Estate
RMB 1250
Romsey-Kerrie Road
ROMSEY
VICTORIA 3434

Fax: 03 5427 0395